CU01561360

aria bites

ONE HUNDRED OPERAS IN HAIKU

TITANIA PEONY PLUME &
TRISTRAM PENDLETON-POET

COPYRIGHT © 2023 TPP LLP
ALL RIGHTS RESERVED.

NO PART OF THIS BOOK CAN BE REPRODUCED IN ANY FORM OR BY WRITTEN, ELECTRONIC OR MECHANICAL, INCLUDING PHOTOCOPYING, RECORDING, OR BY ANY INFORMATION RETRIEVAL SYSTEM WITHOUT WRITTEN PERMISSION IN WRITING BY THE AUTHOR.

PRINTED IN GREAT BRITAIN
ALTHOUGH EVERY PRECAUTION HAS BEEN TAKEN IN THE PREPARATION OF THIS BOOK, THE PUBLISHER AND AUTHOR ASSUME NO RESPONSIBILITY FOR ERRORS OR OMISSIONS. NEITHER IS ANY LIABILITY ASSUMED FOR DAMAGES RESULTING FROM THE USE OF INFORMATION CONTAINED HEREIN.
ISBN 9798394562754

about us

Be introduced to the two wild and wonderful connoisseurs who are taking the world by storm. They love a good tipple, a catchy tune, and a tall tale - but they're not too snooty about it. Along with their discerning taste, they're not afraid to get a little rowdy. In fact, they relish the seedier side of life, just for the fun of it. And let's not forget their feline muse, the one and only Gen. Pussy Talemonger - what a name, what a cat!

Together, they have embarked on a creative journey to write a series of books that are completely random, yet linked by their irreverent humour and general disregard for propriety. They don't care about respectability or purpose - they just want to make you laugh. They've got opinions, they've got humour, and they've got a disregard for the opinions of others - especially their friends. So don't take them too seriously, and don't take yourself too seriously either...just buckle up for a wild ride.

Come and join them on this journey of whimsy and wonder, where the joy of life is celebrated with every page.

Ink whispers of song,

A hundred tales condensed small,

Haiku libretto.

Spring

La Traviata - Giuseppe Verdi
Le Nozze di Figaro - Wolfgang Amadeus Mozart
Don Giovanni - Wolfgang Amadeus Mozart
Così fan tutte - Wolfgang Amadeus Mozart
Faust - Charles Gounod
L'elisir d'amore - Gaetano Donizetti
Lakmé - Léo Delibes
Orfeo ed Euridice - Christoph Willibald Gluck
La fille du régiment - Gaetano Donizetti
Die Entführung aus dem Serail - Wolfgang Amadeus Mozart
Mireille - Charles Gounod
Werther - Jules Massenet
La sonnambula - Vincenzo Bellini
Le roi d'Ys - Édouard Lalo
Manon - Jules Massenet
Der Rosenkavalier - Richard Strauss
La rondine - Giacomo Puccini
The Cunning Little Vixen - Leoš Janáček
The Rake's Progress - Igor Stravinsky
L'amore dei tre re - Italo Montemezzi
The Love for Three Oranges - Sergei Prokofiev
L'enfant et les sortilèges - Maurice Ravel
Albert Herring - Benjamin Britten
Ariadne auf Naxos - Richard Strauss
The Turn of the Screw - Benjamin Britten

Summer

Carmen - Georges Bizet
La bohème - Giacomo Puccini
Aida - Giuseppe Verdi
The Barber of Seville - Gioachino Rossini
Il Trovatore - Giuseppe Verdi
Don Pasquale - Gaetano Donizetti
Les pêcheurs de perles - Georges Bizet
Madama Butterfly - Giacomo Puccini
Cavalleria Rusticana - Pietro Mascagni
La Cenerentola - Gioachino Rossini
Nabucco - Giuseppe Verdi
La Gioconda - Amilcare Ponchielli
Norma - Vincenzo Bellini
I pagliacci - Ruggero Leoncavallo
L'italiana in Algeri - Gioachino Rossini
Die Meistersinger von Nürnberg - Richard Wagner
Rusalka - Antonín Dvořák
I puritani - Vincenzo Bellini
Un ballo in maschera - Giuseppe Verdi
Tannhäuser - Richard Wagner
Pelléas et Mélisande - Claude Debussy
Káťa Kabanová - Leoš Janáček
The Beggar's Opera - John Gay
The Merry Widow - Franz Lehár
Porgy and Bess - George Gershwin

Autumn

Otello – Giuseppe Verdi
Macbeth – Giuseppe Verdi
Tosca – Giacomo Puccini
La fanciulla del West – Giacomo Puccini
Lucia di Lammermoor – Gaetano Donizetti
Eugene Onegin – Pyotr Ilyich Tchaikovsky 7
Rigoletto – Giuseppe Verdi
Boris Godunov – Modest Mussorgsky
Simon Boccanegra – Giuseppe Verdi
Roméo et Juliette – Charles Gounod
The Queen of Spades – Pyotr Ilyich Tchaikovsky
Billy Budd – Benjamin Britten
Jenufa – Leoš Janáček
The Tales of Hoffmann – Jacques Offenbach
La damnation de Faust – Hector Berlioz
Salome – Richard Strauss
Elektra – Richard Strauss
Andrea Chénier – Umberto Giordano
Arabella – Richard Strauss
Don Carlo – Giuseppe Verdi
Die Frau ohne Schatten – Richard Strauss
The Bartered Bride – Bedřich Smetana
Dido and Aeneas – Henry Purcell
Alcina – George Frideric Handel
The Marriage of Figaro – Wolfgang Amadeus Mozart

Winter

Die Fledermaus - Johann Strauss II
The Snow Maiden - Nikolai Rimsky-Korsakov
Hänsel und Gretel - Engelbert Humperdinck
La Wally - Alfredo Catalani
Il tabarro - Giacomo Puccini
Der fliegende Holländer - Richard Wagner
Suor Angelica - Giacomo Puccini
L'arlesiana - Francesco Cilea
The Tsar's Bride - Nikolai Rimsky-Korsakov
Khovanshchina - Modest Mussorgsky
Vanessa - Samuel Barber
The Legend of the Invisible City of Kitezh and the Maiden Fevroniya - Nikolai Rimsky-Korsakov
The Gambler - Sergei Prokofiev
The Fiery Angel - Sergei Prokofiev
Wozzeck - Alban Berg
Dialogues des Carmélites - Francis Poulenc
War and Peace - Sergei Prokofiev
Lulu - Alban Berg
Peter Grimes - Benjamin Britten
Nixon in China - John Adams
Götterdämmerung - Richard Wagner
Das Rheingold - Richard Wagner
Lohengrin - Richard Wagner
Hans Heiling - Heinrich Marschner
Tristan und Isolde - Richard Wagner

Spring

La Traviata

Violetta loves,

Sacrifices self for truth,

Love transcends all bounds.

Giuseppe Verdi
Francesco Maria Piave

Le Nozze di Figaro

Servant outwits lord,
Equality and love win,
Hierarchies crumble.

Wolfgang Amadeus Mozart
Lorenzo Da Ponte

Don Giovanni

Rake pays for his sins,
His end sparks conversation,
Morality's lens.

Wolfgang Amadeus Mozart
Lorenzo Da Ponte

Così fan tutte

Love's fidelity,
Tested, partners switched around,
True love undefined.

Wolfgang Amadeus Mozart
Lorenzo Da Ponte

Faust

Faust's deal with devil,
Gains pleasure, loses his soul,
Defies God's design.

Charles Gounod
Jules Barbier and Michel Carré

L'elisir d'amore

Elixir of love,

False potion, true emotions,

Deception brings truth.

Gaetano Donizetti
Felice Romani

Lakmé

Love crosses divide,
Indian maiden, British man,
Colonial lines blurred.

Léo Delibes
Edmond Gondinet and Philippe Gille

Orfeo ed Euridice

Orpheus defies death,
Love's power breaks convention,
Rules cannot contain.

Christoph Willibald Gluck
Ranieri de' Calzabigi

La fille du régiment

Love knows no station,

Peasant girl, noble soldier,

Class lines dissipate.

Gaetano Donizetti
Jules-Henri Vernoy de Saint-Georges and
Jean-François Bayard

Die Entführung aus dem Serail

Rescue from harem,
Love's strength conquers prejudice,
Cultures intertwined.

Wolfgang Amadeus Mozart
Christoph Friedrich Bretzner
(adapted by Gottlieb Stephanie)

Mireille

Class and love collide,
Mireille defies her father,
Tragic love persists.

Charles Gounod
Michel Carré

Werther

Love unrequited,
Werther's passion undeterred,
Society's norms.

Jules Massenet
Édouard Blau, Paul Milliet, and Georges Hartmann

La sonnambula

Sleepwalker's secret,
Amina's love put to test,
Innocence prevails.

Vincenzo Bellini
Felice Romani

Le roi d'Ys

Sisters' love and strife,
Rivalry for one man's heart,
Dooms a city's fate.

Édouard Lalo
Édouard Blau

Manon

Manon's desires,
Love and wealth in constant strife,
Society's chain.

Jules Massenet
Henri Meilhac and Philippe Gille

Der Rosenkavalier

Age and love compete,

Marschallin yields to youth's grace,

Beauty's fleeting truth.

Richard Strauss
Hugo von Hofmannsthal

La rondine

Love's fleeting promise,

Magda's past and present clash,

Freedom's sacrifice.

Giacomo Puccini
Giuseppe Adami

The Cunning Little Vixen

Vixen's wild spirit,
Nature and man's world entwined,
Freedom's purest form.

Leoš Janáček

The Rake's Progress

Temptation lures Tom,

His downfall serves as warning,

Vice's bitter end.

Igor Stravinsky
W.H. Auden and Chester Kallman

L'amore dei tre re

Love's powerful force,

Three kings, one woman's desire,

Politics and fate.

Italo Montemezzi
Sem Benelli

The Love for Three Oranges

Prince quests for three fruits,

Folly of love revealed, yet,

Defeats cruel witch's plan.

Sergei Prokofiev
Sergei Prokofiev and Vera Janacopoulos

L'enfant et les sortilèges

Child's tantrum unfolds,
Objects and animals speak,
Compassion is learned.

Maurice Ravel
Colette

Albert Herring

Morality's choice,

Albert's reluctant May King,

Freed by defiance.

Benjamin Britten
Eric Crozier

Ariadne auf Naxos

Two worlds intertwine,
Opera and commedia,
Love finds new meaning.

Richard Strauss
Hugo von Hofmannsthal

The Turn of the Screw

Ghosts haunt, children play,
Innocence and darkness meet,
Truth's elusive grasp.

Benjamin Britten
Myfanwy Piper

Summer

Carmen

Fierce Carmen rebels,
Passion and freedom collide,
Defying constraint.

Georges Bizet
Henri Meilhac and Ludovic Halévy

La bohème

Love amidst hardship,
Bohemians choose passion,
Life's fleeting moments.

Giacomo Puccini
Luigi Illica and Giuseppe Giacosa

Aida

Love defies nations,

Aida and Radamès,

Their fate transcends war.

Giuseppe Verdi
Antonio Ghislanzoni

The Barber of Seville

Cunning barber wins,
Love and deception prevail,
Social norms upturned.

Gioachino Rossini
Cesare Sterbini

Il Trovatore

Revenge, love entwined,
Dark secrets come to light, yet,
Justice is defied.

Giuseppe Verdi
Salvadore Cammarano and Leone Emanuele Bardare

Don Pasquale

Age, youth's love contest,
Pasquale tricked and humbled,
Old norms undermined.

Gaetano Donizetti
Giovanni Ruffini

Les pêcheurs de perles

Friendship put to test,
Love for Leïla, loyalty,
Sacrifice prevails.

Georges Bizet
Eugène Cormon and Michel Carré

Madama Butterfly

Tragic Butterfly,
Love betrayed, East meets West, and,
Culture's cruel divide.

Giacomo Puccini
Luigi Illica and Giuseppe Giacosa

Cavalleria Rusticana

Love, betrayal, death,
Sicilian honour code,
Tradition's cruel grip.

Pietro Mascagni
Giovanni Targioni-Tozzetti and Guido Menasci

La Cenerentola

Cinderella's rise,
Kindness, love defeat deceit,
Virtue rewarded.

Gioachino Rossini
Jacopo Ferretti

Nabucco

Babylon's harsh reign,

Abigaille's lust for power,

Faith and love prevail.

Giuseppe Verdi
Temistocle Solera

La Gioconda

Gioconda's self-sacrifice,
Love, envy, tangled desires,
Hidden agendas.

Amilcare Ponchielli
Arrigo Boito

Norma

Druid priestess falls,
Love for enemy, betrayal,
Duty transcended.

Vincenzo Bellini
Felice Romani

I pagliacci

Stage and life entwined,
Canio's laughter turns to tears,
Art's cruel reflection.

Ruggero Leoncavallo

L'italiana in Algeri

Cunning Isabella,

Outsmarts the Bey, love prevails,

Gender roles reversed.

Gioachino Rossini
Angelo Anelli

43

Die Meistersinger von Nürnberg

Artistic freedom,
Wagner's veiled critique of rules,
Tradition defied.

Richard Wagner

Rusalka

Rusalka's great love,
Mortal realm and nature clash,
Price of sacrifice.

Antonín Dvořák
Jaroslav Kvapil

I puritani

Love transcends conflict,
Elvira's heart and loyalty,
Divided no more.

Vincenzo Bellini
Carlo Pepoli

Un ballo in maschera

Love and duty clash,
Gustav's fateful masquerade,
Truth concealed in masks.

Giuseppe Verdi
Antonio Somma

Tannhäuser

Tannhäuser's desires,
Venusberg and Wartburg's strife,
Redemption through love.

Richard Wagner

Pelléas et Mélisande

Mystery, love, fate,
Pelléas and Mélisande,
Truth lies in shadows.

Claude Debussy
Maurice Maeterlinck

Káťa Kabanová

Káťa's love, guilt's weight,
Repression and desire,
Tragic destiny.

Leoš Janáček

The Beggar's Opera

Beggars mock high class,
Satire, love, and crime unite,
Society's flaws.

John Gay

The Merry Widow

Wealth, love, deception,
Merry Widow seeks true match,
Society's game.

Franz Lehár
Viktor Léon and Leo Stein

Porgy and Bess

Porgy and Bess' love,
Trials in Catfish Row unfold,
Strength through adversity.

George Gershwin
DuBose Heyward and Ira Gershwin

Autumn

Otello

Jealousy consumes,
Otello's tragic downfall,
Trust betrayed by lies.

Giuseppe Verdi
Arrigo Boito

Macbeth

Ambition's dark path,
Macbeth and Lady Macbeth,
Greed begets downfall.

Giuseppe Verdi
Francesco Maria Piave

Tosca

Tosca's love and fate,
Betrayal, power, sacrifice,
Despair's final act.

Giacomo Puccini
Luigi Illica and Giuseppe Giacosa

La fanciulla del West

Minnie's love gambled,
Gold Rush passions and dangers,
Forgiveness prevails.

Giacomo Puccini
Guelfo Civinini and Carlo Zangarini

Lucia di Lammermoor

Love lost, madness dawns,
Lucia's heart torn by feuds,
Tragedy unfolds.

Gaetano Donizetti
Salvadore Cammarano

Eugene Onegin

Onegin's cold heart,
Regret and love realised,
Too late for amends.

Pyotr Ilyich Tchaikovsky
Konstantin Shilovsky

Rigoletto

Vengeful Rigoletto,

Love and curses intertwine,

Fate's cruel irony.

Giuseppe Verdi
Francesco Maria Piave

Boris Godunov

Boris' haunted reign,
Guilt, ambition, and power,
Morality's cost.

Modest Mussorgsky

Simon Boccanegra

Boccanegra's plight,
Family, power, and love,
Forgiveness and loss.

Giuseppe Verdi
Francesco Maria Piave and Arrigo Boito

Roméo et Juliette

Love amidst feuds' strife,
Roméo and Juliet,
Death's embrace unites.

Charles Gounod
Jules Barbier and Michel Carré

The Queen of Spades

Gambling hearts and souls,
Gherman's obsession, downfall,
Dark secrets revealed.

Pyotr Ilyich Tchaikovsky
Modest Tchaikovsky

Billy Budd

Billy, innocent,

Claggart's malice, doomed by law,

True justice questioned.

Benjamin Britten
E. M. Forster and Eric Crozier

Jenufa

Love, shame, and secrets,
Jenufa's strength and resolve,
Compassion prevails.

Leoš Janáček

The Tales of Hoffmann

Hoffmann's lost loves,

Reality and fantasy,

Truth in suffering.

Jacques Offenbach
Jules Barbier

La damnation de Faust

Faust's quest for pleasure,
Mephistopheles' dark deal,
Soul's eternal price.

Hector Berlioz
Almire Gandonnière

Salome

Salome's dark dance,
Desire, power, and demise,
Taboo's seduction.

Richard Strauss
Oscar Wilde

Elektra

Elektra's revenge,
Family's murderous past,
Cycle of violence.

Richard Strauss
Hugo von Hofmannsthal

Andrea Chénier

Revolution's rage,
Chénier's love and sacrifice,
Art transcends turmoil.

Umberto Giordano
Luigi Illica

Arabella

Arabella's quest,
Love in a changing era,
True self discovered.

Richard Strauss
Hugo von Hofmannsthal

Don Carlo

Love, power, and fate,
Don Carlo's tragic passion,
Freedom's heavy price.

Giuseppe Verdi
Joseph Méry and Camille du Locle

Die Frau ohne Schatten

Shadowless woman,
Journey through realms of spirit,
Humanity found.

Richard Strauss
Hugo von Hofmannsthal

The Bartered Bride

Marriage bartered, love,
Marenka, Jeník's true bond,
Deceit unravelled.

Bedřich Smetana
Karel Sabina

Dido and Aeneas

Love's fleeting moment,
Dido and Aeneas part,
Sacrifice for fate.

Henry Purcell
Nahum Tate

Alcina

Alcina's island,
Enchantment, love, and deceit,
Truth breaks the spellbound.

George Frideric Handel
Riccardo Broschi

The Marriage of Figaro

Figaro's grand scheme,
Nobility's games unveiled,
Equality's call.

Wolfgang Amadeus Mozart
Lorenzo Da Ponte

Winter

Die Fledermaus

Masquerade of lies,
Eisenstein's mistaken jest,
Truth in revelry.

Johann Strauss II
Karl Haffner and Richard Genée

The Snow Maiden

Snow Maiden's heart yearns,
Love's warmth melts her icy core,
Nature's balance lost.

Nikolai Rimsky-Korsakov

Hänsel und Gretel

Lost in darkened woods,
Hänsel, Gretel face witch's lure,
Innocence prevails.

Engelbert Humperdinck
Adelheid Wette

La Wally

Wally's love, vengeance,
Fateful avalanche consumes,
Nature's harsh decree.

Alfredo Catalani
Luigi Illica

Il tabarro

Barge, love's betrayal,

Michele's vengeance, heartache,

River's dark embrace.

Giacomo Puccini
Giuseppe Adami

Der fliegende Holländer

Cursed Dutchman roams seas,
Senta's love redeems, tragic,
Selflessness unveiled.

Richard Wagner

Suor Angelica

Nun's hidden sorrow,
Angelica's redemption,
Sacrifice for love.

Giacomo Puccini
Giovacchino Forzano

L'arlesiana

Love's obsession, doom,
Federico's heart torn,
Desire's tragic end.

Francesco Cilea
Leopoldo Marenco

The Tsar's Bride

Marfa's love ensnared,
Tsar's bride, poison's cruel twist,
Power's cruel shadow.

Nikolai Rimsky-Korsakov
Ilja Tjumenjev

Khovanshchina

Russian strife, unrest,
Old beliefs clash with the new,
Sacrifice, rebirth.

Modest Mussorgsky

Vanessa

Vanessa's lost love,
Echoes of past haunt the present,
Truth's bitter unveiling.

Samuel Barber
Gian Carlo Menotti

The Legend of the Invisible City of Kitezh and the Maiden Fevroniya

Kitezh, hidden realm,

Fevroniya's pure love,

Mystic salvation..

Nikolai Rimsky-Korsakov
Vladimir Belsky

The Gambler

Gamblers, obsession,

Roulette wheel spins, love and loss,

Fate's cruel reckoning.

Sergei Prokofiev

The Fiery Angel

Renata's visions,
Fiery angel, love, and sin,
Darkness consumes all.

Sergei Prokofiev

Wozzeck

Wozzeck, tragic soul,
Inhumanity laid bare,
World's cruel distortion.

Alban Berg

Dialogues des Carmélites

Nuns defy the state,
Carmélites face guillotine,
Faith's profound courage.

Francis Poulenc

War and Peace

War's devastation,
Love, loyalty, sacrifice,
Humanity's strength.

Sergei Prokofiev
Mira Mendelson

Lulu

Lulu's allure, death,
Morality's dark mirror,
Desire's fatal path.

Alban Berg

Peter Grimes

Grimes, outcast at sea,
Village's scorn, tragic fate,
Judgment's cruel tide.

Benjamin Britten
Montagu Slater

Nixon in China

Nixon, Mao converse,
History's grand stage, human flaws,
Power's subtle dance.

John Adams
Alice Goodman

Götterdämmerung

Twilight of the gods,
Ring's curse, love's betrayal, doom,
Cycle's end, rebirth.

Richard Wagner

Das Rheingold

Ring's power and curse,
Gods and mortals' greed and lust,
Treachery unfolds.

Richard Wagner

Lohengrin

Knight Lohengrin's love,
Trust betrayed, heartache and woe,
Questioned faith's high cost.

Richard Wagner

Hans Heiling

Heiling's heart desires,
Mortal love, unearthly cost,
Loss, redemption's call.

Heinrich Marschner
Eduard Devrient

Tristan und Isolde

Tristan, Isolde,
Love potion's sweet, bitter fate,
Transcendent passion.

Richard Wagner

Printed in Great Britain
by Amazon

4db5c9e8-36f8-4aa5-ad70-baceabc17beeR01